Uncaging Prolific Leadership

Leadership Haikus

by
David Sanders

Uncaging Prolific Leadership
Leadership Haikus
ISBN 978-1-7350180-4-1
Copyright © 2020 David Sanders

Request for information should be addressed to:
Curry Brothers Marketing and Publishing Group
P.O. Box 247 Haymarket, VA 20168

All rights reserved. No part of this publication may be reproduced, stored in a retrieval system, or transmitted in any form or by any means, electronic, mechanical, photocopy, recording, or any other, except for brief quotations in printed reviews, without the prior permission of the publisher.

Cover Design by Romeo Moore

Editing by Joniece Jackson

Behind the Title

Uncaging Prolific Leadership refers to the leader. I have learned each of us at birth are placed in and trapped inside a mental cage, incarcerated by the constructs of our socialization, being set free by her or his own submission to essential life-promoting philosophies.

LEADING YOUNG LEADERS

L Y L

Leading Young Leaders
P.O. Box 681311 Prattville, AL 36808
Contactus@startlyl.com
(443)221-5263
Startlyl.com

What is the "Why"?

Every "why" is either shaped by or affects our future. Young leaders are our future. What better why is there than that?

— David Sanders, Founder

The History

The Leading Young Leaders System was created in response to the founder being denied the ability to teach resilience training to families in low income housing. He prayed about a development opportunity that could promote growth and efficiency in the nation and was led to create the system and its concepts.

What is Leading Young Leaders?

The Five Leadership Disciplines, Vision, Preparation, Communication, Submission, and Growth; Five Young Leader Skills, Communication Engagement Strategy (COES), Partner Recognition and Focus (PRF), Identifying Responsibility (IDR), Productive Transitions (PT), and Stress Appropriation; and the Success Pyramid, Acceptance, Acknowledge, Accelerate, and Achieve are the components that make up the Leading Young Leaders System.

Mission Statement

L.E.A.P.S.A.N.D.B.O.U.N.D.S.
Leaders employing a productive solution and nurturing development by openly uniting, not demoralizing society nor self.

Five Young Leader Skills

Fundamental concepts designed to emerge new and young leaders into the art of leadership. Personal, relational, and organziational domains are all effectively enhanced by these foundational skills.

Five Leadership Disciplines

Institutional practices intended for the initiation, acceleration, combination, consecration, or termination of recurring thoughts, actions, behaviors, practices, and habits. The Five Leadership Disciplines each has three sub-discipline and each sub-discipline has three practices.

Success Pyramid

Requirements each leader must internalize to reach sucess. While success mandates additional elements, the pyramid speaks to areas in which each person, relationship, or organization has intrinsic control.

Our Commitment

Working to power the leadership mastery of young people and new leaders through Education, Inspiration, and Opportunity.

Our Goal is to integrate the Leading Young Leaders system into educational institutions and programs, establish a worldwide foundation of preliminary leadership studies, develop a universal language of leadership, and nurture the development of international partnerships through unity and trust.

Table of Content

Day 1. Effort..3
Day 2. Reality..5
Day 3. Power..7
Day 4 Intelligence...9
Day 5. Vision..11
Day 6. Prepare...13
Day 7. Communicate...15
Day 8. Submission..17
Day 9. Growth..19
Day 10. Partner..21
Day 11. Focus..23
Day 12. Engagement...25
Day 13. Strategy...27
Day 14. Identify...29
Day 15. Responsibility.......................................31
Day 16. Productive...33
Day 17. Transition...35
Day 18. Stress...37
Day 19. Appropriation..39
Day 20. Success..41
Day 21. Acceptance...43
Day 22. Acknowledge..45
Day 23. Accelerate...47

Day 24. Achieve..49
Day 25. Educate...51
Day 26. Inspire...53
Day 27. Opportunity..55
Day 28. Success...57
Day 29. Leadership..59
Day 30. Believe..61
Day 31. Share...63

Introduction
(Before Day 1)

Compelled by the direction of the world around me, I hope to share my source of inspiration to accept the call to acknowledge the requirements for, accelerate towards, and achieve becoming a prolific leader. This book is formatted to offer readers succinct, foundational leadership philosophies to read—daily—with the intent to think, focus, and reflect on personal, relational, and organizational growth. Every person is born with a talent, which means everyone has a purpose and the ability to be magnetic.

As a senior leader in the United States military, Father, and Founder of the Leading Young Leaders System ©, I have been blessed with the opportunity to assist thousands of people with hundreds of issues that threaten growth in their personal and professional lives. These problems regarded stress, conflict, competence, confidence, communication, fear, and so much more.

The philosophies have proven effective in my life and I'm absolutely certain they will do the same for you.

Use this book as a tool for daily meditation and guidance to realize growth in leadership. Make a daily account for what you have done, plan to do and how these practices promote success with goals found in your vision. Repeat this practice upon completion of this book to receive a more dynamic understanding in areas that may have been missed.

Day 1

Effort
Victims and victors —
A victim makes excuses
Be victorious!

"Continuous effort — not strength or intelligence — is the key to unlocking your potential"
— ***Winston Churchill***

Think (How do I perceive this message?)
_____
_____
_____
_____
_____
_____

Reflect (How has this helped, or could have helped, in the past?) _____
_____
_____
_____
_____
_____
_____

Focus (How I will use what I've accepted into current and future leadership practices?)
_____
_____
_____
_____
_____
_____

Day 2

Reality
The pattern matches —
But, the fabric is different
Which is authentic

"Reality leaves a lot to the imagination."

— ***John Lennon***

Think (How do I perceive this message?)
_____
_____
_____
_____
_____
_____

Reflect (How has this helped, or could have helped, in the past?) _____
_____
_____
_____
_____
_____
_____

Focus (How I will use what I've accepted into current and future leadership practices?)
_____
_____
_____
_____
_____
_____

Day 3

Power
Knowledge is power —
No, acceptance is power
Knowledge is chaos

"The day the power of love overrules the love of power, the world will know peace."

— ***Mahatma Gandhi***

Think (How do I perceive this message?)
_____
_____
_____
_____
_____

Reflect (How has this helped, or could have helped, in the past?) _____
_____
_____
_____
_____
_____

Focus (How I will use what I've accepted into current and future leadership practices?)
_____
_____
_____
_____
_____

Day 4

Intelligence
What is the purpose —
Intelligence may cripple
Gain understanding

"I know that I am intelligent, because I know that I know nothing."

— ***Socrates***

Think (How do I perceive this message?)

_____
_____
_____
_____
_____
_____

Reflect (How has this helped, or could have helped, in the past?) _____
_____
_____
_____
_____
_____
_____

Focus (How I will use what I've accepted into current and future leadership practices?)

_____
_____
_____
_____
_____
_____

Day 5

Vision
What one may see now
May never be seen again
How can this happen

"A vision is not just a picture of what could be; it is a call to our better selves, a call to become something more."

— ***Rosabeth Moss Kanter***

Think (How do I perceive this message?)
_____
_____
_____
_____
_____
_____

Reflect (How has this helped, or could have helped, in the past?) _____
_____
_____
_____
_____
_____

Focus (How I will use what I've accepted into current and future leadership practices?)
_____
_____
_____
_____
_____
_____

Day 6

Prepare
Before going out
Take a spiritual journey
Change the atmosphere

"I believe luck is preparation meeting opportunity. If you hadn't been prepared when the opportunity came along, you wouldn't have been lucky."

— Oprah Winfrey

Think (How do I perceive this message?)
_____
_____
_____
_____
_____

Reflect (How has this helped, or could have helped, in the past?) _____
_____
_____
_____
_____
_____

Focus (How I will use what I've accepted into current and future leadership practices?)
_____
_____
_____
_____
_____

Day 7

Communicate
Frequencies collide
What beauty is there to find
Sight beyond the eyes

"Good communication is just as stimulating as black coffee, and just as hard to sleep after."

— ***Anne Morrow Lindbergh***

Think (How do I perceive this message?)
_____
_____
_____
_____
_____
_____

Reflect (How has this helped, or could have helped, in the past?) _____
_____
_____
_____
_____
_____

Focus (How I will use what I've accepted into current and future leadership practices?)
_____
_____
_____
_____
_____
_____

Day 8

Submission
Manifestation —
Discern what receives power
Now give it freely

"We are all servants. The only question is whom we will serve."

— R. C. Sproul

Think (How do I perceive this message?)

_____
_____
_____
_____
_____
_____

Reflect (How has this helped, or could have helped, in the past?) _____
_____
_____
_____
_____
_____

Focus (How I will use what I've accepted into current and future leadership practices?)

_____
_____
_____
_____
_____
_____

Day 9

Growth
What you submit to
Becomes greatest in your life
Make it productive

"Be not afraid of growing slowly; be afraid only of standing still."

— ***Chinese Proverb***

Think (How do I perceive this message?)
_____
_____
_____
_____
_____
_____

Reflect (How has this helped, or could have helped, in the past?) _____
_____
_____
_____
_____
_____

Focus (How I will use what I've accepted into current and future leadership practices?)
_____
_____
_____
_____
_____

Day 10

Partner
He can not get it —
Whenever she comes along
They together can

"Alone we can do so little; together we can do so much."

— Helen Keller

Think (How do I perceive this message?)
_____
_____
_____
_____
_____
_____

Reflect (How has this helped, or could have helped, in the past?) _____
_____
_____
_____
_____
_____
_____

Focus (How I will use what I've accepted into current and future leadership practices?)
_____
_____
_____
_____
_____
_____

Day 11

Focus
Take everything —
Examine it, replace it
Prioritize it

"Lack of direction, not lack of time, is the problem. We all have twenty-four hour days."

— Zig Ziglar

Think (How do I perceive this message?)
_____
_____
_____
_____
_____
_____

Reflect (How has this helped, or could have helped, in the past?) _____
_____
_____
_____
_____
_____

Focus (How I will use what I've accepted into current and future leadership practices?)
_____
_____
_____
_____
_____

Day 12

Engagement
Intend through study
Prepare the lines of effort
Commit to purpose

"Engagement is the offspring of effort and commitment, where we labor and delivery to promote action, cutting the umbilical cord of intent"

— Post Signature

Think (How do I perceive this message?)
_____
_____
_____
_____
_____
_____

Reflect (How has this helped, or could have helped, in the past?) _____
_____
_____
_____
_____
_____

Focus (How I will use what I've accepted into current and future leadership practices?)
_____
_____
_____
_____
_____
_____

Day 13

Strategy
Gain understanding —
Apply pressure as needed
Seize the objective

"Always start at the end before you begin."

— Robert Kiyosaki

Think (How do I perceive this message?)
_____
_____
_____
_____
_____
_____

Reflect (How has this helped, or could have helped, in the past?) _____
_____
_____
_____
_____
_____
_____

Focus (How I will use what I've accepted into current and future leadership practices?)
_____
_____
_____
_____
_____
_____

Day 14

Identify
It barks like a dog
It can even wave its limbs
It must be a tree

"Be yourself; everyone else is already taken."

— ***Oscar Wilde***

Think (How do I perceive this message?)
_____
_____
_____
_____
_____
_____

Reflect (How has this helped, or could have helped, in the past?) _____
_____
_____
_____
_____
_____

Focus (How I will use what I've accepted into current and future leadership practices?)
_____
_____
_____
_____
_____
_____

Day 15

Responsibility
Birthing acceptance
Association conceives
Which one delivers

"Ninety-nine percent of all failures come from people who have a habit of making excuses."

— George Washington Carver

Think (How do I perceive this message?)
_____
_____
_____
_____
_____

Reflect (How has this helped, or could have helped, in the past?) _____
_____
_____
_____
_____
_____

Focus (How I will use what I've accepted into current and future leadership practices?)
_____
_____
_____
_____
_____
_____

Day 16

Productive
Until it gets done —
Wage the greatest war within
Defeat comfort

"Do the hard jobs first. The easy jobs will take care of themselves."

— ***Dale Carnegie***

Think (How do I perceive this message?)
_____
_____
_____
_____
_____
_____

Reflect (How has this helped, or could have helped, in the past?) _____
_____
_____
_____
_____
_____
_____

Focus (How I will use what I've accepted into current and future leadership practices?)
_____
_____
_____
_____
_____
_____

Day 17

Transition
Before you have reached
The beginning of the end
Form future concepts

"Transitions in life can offer opportunities for discovery."

— ***Robbie Shell***

Think (How do I perceive this message?)
_____
_____
_____
_____
_____

Reflect (How has this helped, or could have helped, in the past?) _____
_____
_____
_____
_____
_____

Focus (How I will use what I've accepted into current and future leadership practices?)
_____
_____
_____
_____
_____

Day 18

Stress
Before one can run —
Stress is a requirement
Before one can walk

"This is normal, to have pressure. It's how you respond. Take the pressure, use the pressure, have fun."

— Chan Ho Park

Think (How do I perceive this message?)
_____
_____
_____
_____
_____

Reflect (How has this helped, or could have helped, in the past?) _____
_____
_____
_____
_____
_____

Focus (How I will use what I've accepted into current and future leadership practices?)
_____
_____
_____
_____
_____

Day 19

Appropriation
Something set aside
Insinuates importance
Protected perhaps

"The difference between success and failure is not which stock you buy or which piece of real estate you buy, it's asset allocation."

— *Tony Robbins*

Think (How do I perceive this message?)
_____
_____
_____
_____
_____

Reflect (How has this helped, or could have helped, in the past?) _____
_____
_____
_____
_____
_____

Focus (How I will use what I've accepted into current and future leadership practices?)
_____
_____
_____
_____
_____

Day 20

Success
Vision now realized
Courage determines the size
Process wills the prize

"The real test is not whether you avoid this failure, because you won't. It's whether you let it harden or shame you into inaction, or whether you learn from it; whether you choose to persevere."

— Barack Obama

Think (How do I perceive this message?)
_____
_____
_____
_____
_____
_____

Reflect (How has this helped, or could have helped, in the past?) _____
_____
_____
_____
_____
_____
_____

Focus (How I will use what I've accepted into current and future leadership practices?)
_____
_____
_____
_____
_____
_____

Day 21

Acceptance
Submit to the way —
Pride becomes the enemy
Of accomplishment

"For after all, the best thing one can do when it is raining is let it rain."

– Henry Wadsworth Longfellow

Think (How do I perceive this message?)
_____
_____
_____
_____

Reflect (How has this helped, or could have helped, in the past?) _____
_____
_____
_____
_____

Focus (How I will use what I've accepted into current and future leadership practices?)
_____
_____
_____
_____
_____

Day 22

Acknowledge
More than awareness —
A higher level response
Is appropriate

"Whatever you acknowledge gains the legitimacy to exist within your world."

— Steven Redhead

Think (How do I perceive this message?)
_____
_____
_____
_____
_____

Reflect (How has this helped, or could have helped, in the past?) _____
_____
_____
_____
_____
_____

Focus (How I will use what I've accepted into current and future leadership practices?)
_____
_____
_____
_____
_____

Day 23

Accelerate
Progress to the goal —
Sometimes slowing a thing down
Gets us there faster

"Positive attitude accelerates your development as a creative person. Believe in yourself."

— Nita Leland

Think (How do I perceive this message?)
_____
_____
_____
_____
_____

Reflect (How has this helped, or could have helped, in the past?) _____
_____
_____
_____
_____
_____

Focus (How I will use what I've accepted into current and future leadership practices?)
_____
_____
_____
_____
_____

Day 24

Achieve
Greater than winning —
Achievement is personal
Enjoyed from within

"Things work out best for those who make the best of how things work out."

— John Wooden

Think (How do I perceive this message?)
_____
_____
_____
_____
_____

Reflect (How has this helped, or could have helped, in the past?) _____
_____
_____
_____
_____
_____

Focus (How I will use what I've accepted into current and future leadership practices?)
_____
_____
_____
_____
_____
_____

Day 25

Educate
Learn, unlearn, relearn —
Understand the circumstance
As life transitions

"The only person who is educated is the one who has learned how to learn, and change."

— ***Carl Rogers***

Think (How do I perceive this message?)
_____
_____
_____
_____
_____

Reflect (How has this helped, or could have helped, in the past?) _____
_____
_____
_____
_____
_____

Focus (How I will use what I've accepted into current and future leadership practices?)
_____
_____
_____
_____
_____

Day 26

Inspire
Aroused assurance —
Provide reason for action
Towards desire

"Learn to light a candle in the darkest moments of someone's life. Be the light that helps others see; it is what gives life its deepest significance."

— Roy T. Bennett

Think (How do I perceive this message?)
_____
_____
_____
_____
_____
_____

Reflect (How has this helped, or could have helped, in the past?) _____
_____
_____
_____
_____
_____

Focus (How I will use what I've accepted into current and future leadership practices?)
_____
_____
_____
_____
_____

Day 27

Opportunity
Fueled by submission —
Through nature, grace, or mercy
To one's own avail

"Someone's sitting in the shade today because someone planted a tree a long time ago."

— Warren Buffett

Think (How do I perceive this message?)
_____
_____
_____
_____
_____
_____

Reflect (How has this helped, or could have helped, in the past?) _____
_____
_____
_____
_____
_____
_____

Focus (How I will use what I've accepted into current and future leadership practices?)
_____
_____
_____
_____
_____

Day 28

Success
An accepted end —
By phase or totality
Where a goal is reached

"Many of life's failures are people who did not realize how close they were to success when they gave up."

— Thomas Edison

Think (How do I perceive this message?)
_____
_____
_____
_____
_____
_____

Reflect (How has this helped, or could have helped, in the past?) _____
_____
_____
_____
_____
_____
_____

Focus (How I will use what I've accepted into current and future leadership practices?)
_____
_____
_____
_____
_____
_____

Day 29

Leadership
Bringing together
The people and resources
To achieve success

"The growth and development of people is the highest calling of leadership."

— Harvey S. Firestone

Think (How do I perceive this message?)
_____
_____
_____
_____
_____

Reflect (How has this helped, or could have helped, in the past?) _____
_____
_____
_____
_____
_____

Focus (How I will use what I've accepted into current and future leadership practices?)
_____
_____
_____
_____
_____

Day 30

Believe
For you to become
Led into a new being
You must first believe

"Therefore I tell you, whatever you ask for in prayer, believe that you have received it, and it will be yours."

— *Jesus*

Think (How do I perceive this message?)

_____
_____
_____
_____
_____
_____

Reflect (How has this helped, or could have helped, in the past?) _____

_____
_____
_____
_____
_____
_____

Focus (How I will use what I've accepted into current and future leadership practices?)

_____
_____
_____
_____
_____
_____

Day 31

Share
Knowing when to give
At the expense of ourselves
For a greater cause

"Life's most persistent and urgent question is, 'What are you doing for others?"

— Dr. Martin Luther King Jr.

Think (How do I perceive this message?)
_____
_____
_____
_____
_____
_____

Reflect (How has this helped, or could have helped, in the past?) _____
_____
_____
_____
_____
_____

Focus (How I will use what I've accepted into current and future leadership practices?)
_____
_____
_____
_____
_____
_____

Thank You!

Heavenly Father, thank you so very much for speaking clearly to my heart and increasing my desire to do your will. Thank you for the comfort in my discomfort and the courage and wisdom to accept others that have helped me along the way. I thank you for Dr. Gerald Curry's friendship, guidance, care, and support. I thank you for my wife and the experiences we have shared that have influenced my growth. Thank you for my children, each as individuals; they reinforce my why. Thank you Lord for my mother! She has been my rock and example of what it means to persevere, with kindness, even when I don't feel a person deserves it. Lastly, thank you for my sister and second mom, Faye; only you know the love and adoration I have for her. I pray that they are all blessed and covered in your love.

Welcome to the Curry family. Got an idea for a book? Contact Curry Brothers Marketing and Publishing Group, LLC. We are not satisfied until your publishing dreams come true. We specialize in all genres of books, especially religion, leadership, family history, poetry, and children's literature. There is an African Proverb that confirms, *"When an elder dies, a library closes."* We advise, be careful who tells your family history. Are their values your family's values? Our staff will navigate you through the entire publishing process, and we take pride in going the extra mile by exceeding your publishing goals.

Improving the world one book at a time!

Curry Brothers Publishing, LLC
PO Box 247
Haymarket, VA 20168
(719) 466-7518 & (615) 347-9124
Visit us at www.currybrotherspublishing.com

www.ingramcontent.com/pod-product-compliance
Lightning Source LLC
Chambersburg PA
CBHW042119100526
44587CB00025B/4121